# RESEARCH METHODOLOGY

OYOVWI M. OBUKOHWO

Made with ♥ on the Notion Press Platform
www.notionpress.com

To Debbie-karine, Mela-D'mata and Tehi-elect as well as my beautiful wife. I have nothing but gratitude to you, my children and wife, for reminding me that walking to the beach is just as fun as being there.

# Contents

# Foreword

Research is simply the methodical analysis of materials and sources to draw inferences. It was around long before it was defined in books like this one, and it will continue to be around long after this course ends. A fascinating species, humans are. We are constantly looking for fresh approaches to tasks as well as ways to enhance current procedures. That needs investigation. Consequently, this book serves as a useful introduction to research methodology. It's likely not the final book you'll need to read on the subject if you plan to conduct research for a degree or a career. With a focus on the comprehension of research technique and practical applications of the knowledge, this is meant to be somewhat of a light introduction.

We hope that this book will contribute to that understanding and enhance your research methodology. Please let us know if you have any ideas for this book's enhancements or if you'd like to see a test added.

Mrs Rotu A. Rume (B.Sc, Delsu; M.Sc, UI)

# Preface

This book is designed to introduce students to the process of scientific research in the social sciences, business, education, public health, and related disciplines. This book is based on my lecture materials developed over a decade of teaching on Research Methods at the University. The target audience for this book includes students, junior researchers, and professors teaching courses on research methods, although senior researchers can also use this book as a handy and compact reference.

However, I plan to continually update this book based on emerging trends in scientific research. If there are any new or interesting content that you wish to see in future editions, please drop me a note, and I will try my best to accommodate them. Comments, criticisms, or corrections to any of the existing content will also be gratefully appreciated.

Oyovwi Mega O
Megalect@gmail.com
09055158093 & 08066096369

# Acknowledgements

It's more difficult and fulfilling than I could have ever anticipated to write a book. Without God and my adorable wife, none of this would be possible. I want to thank God most of all since I couldn't do all of this without Him. I also like to thank Rume A, my wonderful wife. She was just as crucial to the completion of this book as I was, reading early manuscripts, offering suggestions for the cover, and keeping the munchkins out of my hair while I edited. Thank you very much, sweetheart.

# Prologue

Research methods are the instruments and procedures used to do research. Any type of investigation meant to unearth intriguing or novel data falls within the broad definition of research. As with all activities, the level of rigor used in this activity will be reflected in the caliber of the outcomes. This book provides a fundamental overview of the nature of research and the methods that are used to conduct a variety of investigations pertinent to a wide range of subjects, including the natural sciences, social science, social anthropology, psychology, politics, leisure studies and sport, hospitality, healthcare and nursing studies, the environment, business, education, and the humanities. The amount of independent research that students are required to complete for projects, dissertations, and theses in almost every university subject increases with the level of education. As a result, this book presents an in-depth and complete perspective on research as a method for logical problem-solving. It is based on the philosophical-pragmatic tenet that information and research processes have value when applied to the real world. The book is therefore organized into six Chapters and gives an overview of research ethics, project and design, proposal, writing thesis, and general Useful Tool for Findings Purpose in addition to information on the experimental basis of presenting your research in a clear and appealing way.

CHAPTER ONE

# BASIC AND APPLIED RESEARCH

## INTRODUCTION

Research is a serious academic activity with a set of objectives to explain or analyse or understand a problem or finding solution(s) for the problem(s) by adopting a systematic approach in collecting, organizing and analyzing the information relating to the problem. The process of research came into being due to man's quest to be at tune with his environment and also understand nature. To achieve this, man uses the tools of experience and reasoning available to him. Man also makes use of experience and authoritative sources beyond his immediate circle. Experience and authority are rich and major sources of hypothesis, which are based mainly on common sense knowledge and haphazard events, therefore it can be unjustified for drawing conclusions on events. Hence research hypothesis formulation using experience and authority is judged to be unscientific. Research anchors on scientific reasoning; which could be inductive and deductive or both. Research is a combination of both experience and reasoning and can be said to be the most appropriate way of discovering the truth, precisely in the natural Sciences.

The need to research came due to the following reason:

1. To acquire a degree
2. To get respectability
3. To face a challenge
4. To solve a problem
5. To get Intellectual Joy
6. To Serve Society by increasing Standard of living for Science and technology and by Showing the right path to society in case of social and behavioural Sciences.

## DEFINITION OF RESEARCH

There can be many definitions of research. These are provided below:

- Research is an activity of systematic enquiry that seeks answers to a problem.
- Research is a scientific inquiry aimed at learning new facts, testing ideas, etc. It is the systematic collection, analysis and interpretation of data to generate new knowledge and answer a certain question or solve a problem.
- Research in common parlance refers to a search for knowledge.
- According to Clifford Woody research comprises defining and redefining problems, formulating hypothesis or suggested solutions; collecting, organizing and evaluating data; making deductions and reaching conclusions; and at last carefully testing the conclusions to determine whether they fit the formulating hypothesis.
- research is defined as a movement, a movement from the known to the unknown. It is an effort to discover something.
- Research may also be defined ”Any organized enquiry discussed and carried out to provide information for solving a problem”.
- Research is a discipline inquiring which must be conducted and reported so that its logical argument can be carefully examined

## RESEARCH AS A PROCESS

Research can be seen as a series of linked activities moving from a beginning to an end. Research usually begins with the identification of a problem followed by formulation of research questions or objectives. Proceeding from this the researcher determines how best to answer these questions and so decides what information to collect, how it will be collected, and how it will be analysed in order to answer the research question. Regardless of the route taken subsequently, research should start with the problem and the research questions. If the intention of research is to answer your questions, it follows that choice of method should develop from your question: choose the method that can best provide the information you need to answer your research question given the resources available to you. This is one reason why it is very important to be clear as to what you are asking. There are numerous choices to be made within the research process such as

- Identification of problem, i.e., discovering and defining a specific problem within the area one choose to study.
- Planning and organizing for a solution which involve formulating a set of hypotheses, developing operational definitions, formulating a research design and identifying and constructing devices for observation and measurement.
- Conducting the study
- Documentation which entails writing a thesis or desertation based on finding.
- Oral defence of the thesis or desertation.
- Publication of the findings in appropriate outlets

However,. Planning your research involves the consideration of four overlapping themes.

- The conceptual approach –the philosophical underpinnings of research
- Research design –how data collection is organized
- Data collection techniques –how data are collected
- Sampling –from whom data are collected

## CHARACTERISTICS OF RESEARCH

- It demands a clear statement of the problem
- It requires a plan (it is not aimlessly " looking" for something in the hope that you will come across a solution)
- It builds on existing data, using both positive and negative findings
- New data should be collected as required and be organized in such a way that they answer the research question(s)

## PURPOSE OF CONDUCTING RESEARCH

Research serves many purposes. Three of the most common and useful purposes, however, are

exploration, description, and explanation. However, the purpose of research seeks;

- To develop focus
- To reveal characteristics of individual or situation or a group
- To determine frequencies of occurrency

- To test hypothesis
- To increase knowledge within discipline
- To increase knowledge within oneself as a professional consumerof research in order evaluateand apprehend new development within discipline

**QUALITIES OF A GOOD ACADEMIC RESEARCH**

Academic Research is defined as a process of collecting, analyzing and interpreting information to answer questions or solve a problem. A research is a comprehensive task and it requires great effort as a researcher on your part. The first thing that determines the success of your research is your research topic. A good research method should lead to

- Originality/ Novelty
- Contribution to knowledge
- Significance
- Technical soundness
- Critical assessment of existing work

More elaborately, A good research topic should have the following qualities.

1. **Clarity:** This is the most important quality of any research topic. The topic should have to be clear so that others can easily understand the nature of your research. The research topic should have a single interpretation so that people cannot get distracted. The topic should have to be very clear in your mind so that you can properly undertake it. The research topic should have to be free of any ambiguity. Clarity also means that the research topic should have to be directional and it should set the whole research methadology.
2. **Well-defined** and well-phrased research topic is a half guarantee of a successful research. Sometimes researchers phrase the research topic in such a way that it gives a double-barrelled impression. The research topic should have to be well-defined and well-phrased and it should have to be easy to understand. it should have a single meaning.
3. **The language** of the research topic should have to be simple. You should use technical terms only when it is necessary, otherwise use simple words so that everyone can understand it. keep the ethics of writing in

your mind to avoid any unethical term or sentence. Do not introduce any sort of bias directly or indirectly, willingly or unwillingly in the research problem or research topic.

4. **The titling** of the research problem should follow the rules of titling. there are various rules of titling. You can either use a sentence case or a title case but most of the titles follow title case. Read the rules of titling titles before writing it down.
5. **Current importance** should also be the consideration of the researcher while selecting a research topic. An obsolete topic will not be beneficial for anyone the topic should have current importance. You should also assess how much the topic will provide benefit to the field in which you are conducting the study.
6. **Citation:** It should be based on the work of others.
7. **Replicated:**It should be replicated, doable and transmittable .
8. **Logical:** It should based on some logical rationale and tied to theory. In a way that it has the potential to suggest directions for future research.
9. It generates new questions or is cyclical in nature.
10. It should be incremental.
11. **Valid:** Valid and verifiable such that whatever you conclude on the basis of your findings is correct and can be verified by you and others.
12. The researcher is sincerely interested and/or invested in this research.
13. The research should be honest in reporting the facts and revealing the flaws in the work.

## CLASSIFICATIONOF RESEARCH

Research can be classified either as the following;

**Basic Research**: Basic research is mostly conducted to enhance knowledge. It covers fundamental aspects of research. The main motivation of this research is knowledge expansion. It is a non-commercial research and doesn't facilitate in creating or inventing anything. For example, an experiment is a good example of basic research.

**Applied Research**: Applied research focuses on analyzing and solving real-life problems. This type of research refers to the study that helps solve practical problems using scientific methods. This research plays an important role in solving issues that impact the overall well-being of humans. For example, finding a specific cure for a disease.

**Obtrusive research** - where the researcher introduces conditions that influence participants. Where the researcher manipulates the environment.

**Non-obtrusive research** - where researcher avoids influencing subjects in any way and tries to be as inconspicuous as possible.

**TYPES OF RESEARCH**

Research is a systematic search for information and new knowledge. It covers topics in every field of science and perceptions of its scope and activities are unlimited. The classical broad divisions of research are:.

**Problem Oriented Research:** As the name suggests, problem-oriented research is conducted to understand the exact nature of the problem to find out relevant solutions. The term "problem" refers to having issues or two thoughts while making any decisions. For example, Revenue of a car company has decreased by 12% in the last year. The following could be the probable causes: There is no optimum production, poor quality of a product, no advertising, economic conditions etc.

**Problem Solving Research**: This type of research is conducted by companies to understand and resolve their own problems. The problem-solving research uses applied research to find solutions to the existing problems.

**Qualitative research: This** is concerned with developing explanations of social phenomena. That is to say, it aims to help us to understand the world in which we live and why things are the way they are. It is concerned with the social aspects of our world and seeks to answer questions about:

- Why people behave the way they do
- How opinions and attitudes are formed
- How people are affected by the events that go on around them
- How and why cultures have developed in the way they have

Qualitative research is concerned with finding the answers to questions which begin with: why? How? In what way?

**Quantitative Research:**Qualitative research is a structured way of collecting data and analyzing it to draw conclusions. Unlike qualitative research, this research method uses a computational, statistical and similar method to collect and analyze data. Quantitative data is all about numbers. Quantitative research involves a larger population as more number of people means more data. In this manner, more data can be analyzed to obtain accurate results. This type of research method uses close-ended questions because, in quantitative research, the researchers are typically looking at measuring the extent and gathering foolproof statistical data. Online surveys, questionnaires, and polls are preferable data collection tools used in quantitative research. There are various methods of deploying surveys or questionnaires. In recent times online surveys and questionnaires have gained popularity. Survey respondents can receive these surveys on mobile phones, emails or can simply use the internet to access surveys or questionnaires. Quantitative research, on the other hand, is more concerned with questions about: how much? How many? How often? To what extent? etc

**Historical Research:** A systematic process of searching for information and fact to describe analyze or interpret the past

**Ethnographic Research:** This is the systemic process that analyze current situation. It involves -in-depth analytical description of educational systems, processes, and phenomena within a specific context based on detailed observations and interviews -detailed examination of a single group, individual, situation, or site is called a case study

**Experimental Research:** An experiment is a research situation where at least one independent variable, called the experimental variable, is deliberately manipulated or varied by the researcher.

**Ex post facto/Causal comparative Research**: It identifies an effect that has already occurred and attempts to infer cause.Here, a treatment variable (alleged cause) is identified (but not manipulated) and effects are measured; a groups exposed to the treatment variable are compared to groups who are not. The identification of cause can be called into question because groups were not randomly assigned and other extraneous variables were not controlled

**Correlation Research:** The purpose is to find relationships between two or more variable so to: -Better understand the conditions and events that we encounter (what goes with what).

-To predict future conditions and events.

-Correlations do not show cause and effect.

**Descriptive Research:** This is focuses on throwing more light on current issues through a process of data collection. Descriptive studies are used to describe the behavior of a sample population. In descriptive research, only one variable (anything that has quantity or quality that varies) is required to conduct a study. The three main purposes of descriptive research are describing, explaining and validating the findings. For example, a research conducted to know if top-level management leaders in the 21st century posses the moral right to receive a huge sum of money from the company profit?

**Explanatory Research:** Explanatory research or causal research, is conducted to understand the impact of certain changes in existing standard procedures. Conducting experiments is the most popular form of casual research. For example, research conducted to understand the effect of rebranding on customer loyalty.

**Conceptual Research.** Conceptual research : is that related to some abstract idea(s) or theory.

**Empirical Research:** Empirical research ; It is data-based research, coming up with conclusions which are capable of being verified by observation or experiment. We can also call it as experimental type of research.

**Other Types of Research:**

One-time research or longitudinal research. In the former case the research is confined to a single time-period, whereas in the latter case the research is carried on over several time-periods.

Field-setting research or laboratory research or simulation research, depending upon the environment in which it is to be carried out.

Clinical or diagnostic research: Such research follow case-study methods or in-depth approaches to reach the basic causal relations.

Conclusion-oriented and decision-oriented Research: While doing conclusion-oriented research, a researcher is free to pick up a problem, redesign the enquiry as he proceeds and is prepared to conceptualize as he wishes.

**IMPORTANCE OF RESEARCH**

The role of research is important in all fields, in a similar manner, the importance of research is very vital. This is because of various reasons like:

- It serves as tool for building nnowledge and for facilitating learning
- It gives the systematic analysis of the topic
- It Leads to great observations
- It Results in predictions, theories, and many principles
- It improving practices Helps in initiating the action
- It helps in development of new understanding related to the learning, teaching
- It Helps in decision making
- It brings consistency in the work
- It helps to create a balance between the collaborative and individual work

- It helps in understanding the society
- It serves as a tool for enhancing human capital development
- It helps in knowing the culture
- It serves as means to Understand Various Issues and Increase Public Awareness
- It serves as way to Prove Lies and to Support Truths
- It is means to find, gauge, and seize opportunities

**CHALLENGINGS OF RESEARCH**

There are many challenges that inhibit carrying out meaningful research study in the nation's tertiary institutions. These clogs in the wheel of progress include:

- Lack of funds for research
- Lack of information network
- Poor infrastrunctural management
- Ineffective library system
- Ineffective educational system
- Low accessibility to data and information
- Incessant power supply
- Lack of equipment, facilities and material

CHAPTER TWO

# RESEARCH ETHICS

According to Webster's Ninth New Collegiate Dictionary, Ethics can be define as follows

- The discipline of dealing with what is good and bad, with moral duty and obligation
- A set of moral principles or values
- The principle of conduct governing an individual or group

However, Research Ethics can be defined as the application of moral rules and professional codes of conduct to the collection, collation, analysis, report, and dissemination of information about research animal or subjects, especially as related to active acceptance of subjects' right to privacy, confidentiality, and informed consent.

Research ethics are the adherence to certain morality conducts imposed on researchers required by certain research institutions or universities. Research ethics govern the standards of conduct for scientific researchers. It is important to adhere to ethical principles in order to protect the dignity, rights and welfare of research participants.

As such, all research involving human beings should be reviewed by an ethics committee to ensure that the appropriate ethical standards are being upheld. More so, there are different categories of human subject research. This includes

1. Unhealthy human participant or patients for clinical trials of new drugs/ devices
2. Healthy human participant volunteers for clinical trials of new drugs/ devices
3. Tissues and Blood

4. Aggregate data and patient charts
5. Genetic interventions on non-Human species

The reasons for the use of the above various Human subjects categories are

1. Formulation of public health safety issues for the well being of humans
2. To study diseases
3. For testing and development of new treatment pattern to combat diseases

There are a number of **ethical principles** that should be taken into account when performing research. These are;

**Beneficence:**

Beneficence is action that is done for the benefit of others. This principle states that research should do*no harm and Maximize benefits for participants and minimize risks for participants.* There are a number of types of harm that participants can be subjected to. These include:

- Physical harm to participants.
- Psychological distress and discomfort.
- Social disadvantage.
- Harm to participants? financial status.
- An invasion of participants? privacy and anonymity.

When conducting research on human subjects, minimize harms and risks and maximize benefits; respect human dignity, privacy, and autonomy.

**Justice:**

This principle deals with the concept of fairness. This encompasses issues related to who benefits from research and who bears the risks of research. It provides the framework for thinking about these decisions in ways that are fair and equitable. The principle of justice also indicates that questions being asked in trials should be of relevance to the communities participating in the study.

**Informed consent:**

One of the foundations of research ethics is the idea of **informed consent**. Thus, **informed consent** means that participants should understand that they are taking part in research and what the research requires of them. Such information may include the purpose of the research, the methods being used, the possible outcomes of the research, as well as associated demands, discomforts, inconveniences and risks that the participants may face. Another component of informed consent is the principle that participants should be **volunteers**, taking part without having been **coerced** and **deceived.**

**Honesty:**

Honestly report data, results, methods and procedures, and publication status. Do not fabricate, falsify, or misrepresent data.

**Objectivity:**

Strive to avoid bias in experimental design, data analysis, data interpretation, peer review, personnel decisions, grant writing, expert testimony, and other aspects of research.

**Integrity:**

Keep your promises and agreements; act with sincerity; strive for consistency of thought and action.

**Carefulness:**

Avoid careless errors and negligence; carefully and critically examine your own work and the work of your peers. Keep good records of research activities.

**Openness:**

Share data, results, ideas, tools, resources. Be open to criticism and new ideas.

**Respect for Intellectual Property:**

Honor patents, copyrights, and other forms of intellectual property. Do not use unpublished data, methods, or results without permission. Give credit where credit is due. Never plagiarize.

**Confidentiality:**

Protect confidential communications, such as papers or grants submitted for publication, personnel records, trade or military secrets, and patient records.

**Responsible Publication:**

Publish in order to advance research and scholarship, not to advance just your own career. Avoid wasteful and duplicative publication.

**Responsible Mentoring:**

Help to educate, mentor, and advise students. Promote their welfare and allow them to make their own decisions.

**Respect for Colleagues:**

Respect your colleagues and treat them fairly.

**Social Responsibility:**

Strive to promote social good and prevent or mitigate social harms through research, public education, and advocacy.

**Non-Discrimination:**

Avoid discrimination against colleagues or students on the basis of sex, race, ethnicity, or other factors that are not related to their scientific competence and integrity.

**Competence:**

Maintain and improve your own professional competence and expertise through lifelong education and learning; take steps to promote competence in science as a whole.

**Legality:**

Know and obey relevant laws and institutional and governmental policies.

**Animal Care:**

Show proper respect and care for animals when using them in research. Do not conduct unnecessary or poorly designed animal experiments.

**IMPORTANT OF ETHICS OF RESEARCH**

There are several reasons why it is important to adhere to ethical norms in research.

- First, norms promote the aims of research, such as knowledge, truth, and avoidance of error.
- For example, prohibitions against fabricating, falsifying, or misrepresenting research data promote the truth and minimize error.

CHAPTER THREE

# RESEARCH PROJECT AND DESIGN

**WHAT IS RESEARCH PROJECT?**

A research projects is a systematic, structured study to address a specific problem. It encompasses a set interrelated period of time with the aim of producing a producing a specified product. The research process as earlier discussed involves:

- Identify the problem,
- Examining selected relevant variables,
- Formulating hypothesis where appropriate and possible,
- Developing a research design
- Conducting experiments to test the hypothesis,
- Collecting relevant data
- Analyzing the results using statistical software (SPSS & Graphpad)
- Discussing the results
- Drawing appropriate conclusions

Research data can be collected by any one or more of the following ways:

**i. By observation:** This approach suggests that information will be gathered by the investigator's own observation, rather than through speaking with the respondents. The information gathered is relevant to the present and is not complicated by the respondents' past actions, future intentions, or views. There is no doubt that this procedure is expensive, and it also yields very little information. As a result, this approach is inappropriate for studies involving large samples..

**ii. Through personal interview:** The investigator follows a strict process and uses in-person interviews to gather information in order to address a set of preconceived questions. This approach of gathering data is typically conducted in a systematic manner, where output greatly depends on the interviewer's skill.

**iii.Through telephone interviews:** This method of information gathering entails calling the respondents directly. Although not very popular, this technique is crucial for industrial surveys in industrialized regions, especially when there is a short window of time to complete the survey.

**iv. By mailing of questionnaires:** If this approach to surveying is used, the researcher and the respondents do interact. Respondents receive questionnaires in the mail, with instructions to return them once they are finished. The majority of economic and business surveys use this technique. Before using this method, a pilot study is typically conducted to test the questionnaire, which identifies any shortcomings the questionnaire may have. The questionnaire that will be utilized needs to be carefully constructed if it is to be successful in gathering the necessary data.

**v. Through schedules:** The enumerators are chosen and trained using this manner. Schedules with pertinent questions are given to them. These enumerators deliver these schedules to the respondents. On the basis of the responses provided by respondents, enumerators complete out the schedules to gather the data. Regarding this strategy, a lot depends on how capable the enumerators are. To ensure earnest effort, the enumerators' work may undergo sporadic field inspections.

**WHAT IS RESEARCH DESIGN?**

The research designer understandably cannot hold all his decisions in his head. Even if he could, he would have difficulty in understanding how these are inter-related. Therefore, he records his decisions on paper or record disc by using relevant symbols or concepts. Such a symbolic construction may be called the research design or model. A**research design**is a systematic approach that a researcher uses to conduct a scientific study. It is the overall synchronization of identified components and data resulting in a plausible outcome. To conclusively come up with an authentic and accurate result, the research design should follow a strategic methodology, in line with the type of research chosen. To have a better understanding of which research paper topic, to begin with, it is imperative to first identify the types of research to start writing a research proposal.

**COMPONENTS OF RESEARCH DESIGN**

It is important to be familiar with the important concepts relating to research design. They are:

- Dependent and Independent variables
- Extraneous variable
- Control
- Confounded relationship.

**TYPES OF RESEARCH DESIGN**

There are four types of research designs which are:

- **Exploratory Research**: Just as the word implies, it explores, that is to find out about something by answering the question in "what" or "How" manner.
- **Descriptive Research**: This is more in-depth research, which answered the question what and how.
- **Explanatory Research**: This seeks to explain the subject matter being researched and tries to answer the question what, how and why.
- **Evaluation Research**: This is quite extensive as it measures the effectiveness of a program.

With a clear understating of the types of research designs, design research can be drawn. Just like the way an architect chooses a layout from its many designs to fit a specific landscape, the same way a research design is picked from the many designs to fit the type of research being carried out.

On a general term, research design is viewed from two perspectives, a quantitative research design or a qualitative research design, which both have extended components. They can both be used or applied distinctively or together.

**WHAT IS QUANTITATIVE RESEARCH DESIGN?**

A quantitative research design is used to examine the relationship between variable by using numbers and statistics to explain and analyze its findings and there are four types of quantitative research design:

- **Descriptive design research**: As the name implies, it is intended to describe the present status of a This type of design does not require a hypothesis to begin with. These analyses are generated from existing data.

- **Correlational design research:** This seeks to discover If two variables are associated or related in some way, using statistical analysis, while observing the variable.
- **Experimental design research:** This is a method used to establish a cause and effect relationship between two variables or among a group of variables. The independent variable is manipulated to observe the effect on the depended variable. For example, a certain group is exposed to a variable and then compared with the group not exposed to the variable.
- **Quasi-experimental design research:** This experiment is designed just like the true experimental design, except that it does not use randomized sample groups. Also, it is used when a typical research design is not practicable.

### WHAT IS QUALITATIVE RESEARCH DESIGN?

Qualitative research design, on the other hand, is exploratory in nature as it tries to explore not predict the outcome. It seeks to answer the questions what and how. A *qualitative research design* is used to explore the meaning and understanding of complex social environments, like the nature of people's experience, using case studies. A *quantitative research design* shares similar characteristics with scientific research in the following ways.

- An outline question stating the problem that needs to be solved.
- Has a set order and procedure used to answer these questions?
- Analyses the data generated.
- Draws its conclusion after the data has been collated and analyzed so that the conclusion drawn from the findings are not predetermined.

Besides the similarities identified above, a *qualitative research design* also intends to understand, describe or discover the findings. The researcher is usually the primary instrument that formulates the question and interprets the meaning of a data. The data used are mostly documented words from interview, newspapers videos etc. More than one type of data is collected during this research, from the field, where the participants are. In other words, the research goes beyond the intended scope, so making it emergent because the method of research changes and different types of data might be collected as the research goes on.

## NEED FOR RESEARCH DESIGN

Research design is needed because it facilitates the smooth sailing of the various research operations, thereby making research as efficient as possible yielding maximal information with minimal expenditure of effort, time and money.

## FEATURES OF A GOOD RESEARCH DESIGN

A research design appropriate for a particular research problem, usually involves the consideration of the following factors:

i. The means of obtaining information;
ii. The availability and skills of the researcher and his staff, if any.
iii. The objective of the problem to be studied.
iv. The nature of the problem to be studied.
v. The availability of time and money for the research work.

## BASIC PRINCIPLES OF EXPERIMENTAL DESIGNS

Professor Fisher has enumerated three principles of experimental designs:

(1) **The Principle of Replication:** According to the Principle of Replication, the experiment should be repeated more than once. Thus, each treatment is applied in many experimental units instead of one. By doing so the statistical accuracy of the experiments is increased. For example, suppose we are to examine the effect of two varieties of rice. For this purpose we may divide the field into two parts and grow one variety in one part and the other variety in the other part. We can then compare the yield of the two parts and draw conclusion on that basis. But if we are to apply the principle of replication to this experiment, then we first divide the field into several parts, grow one variety in half of these parts and the other variety in the remaining parts. We can then collect the data of yield of the two varieties and draw conclusion by comparing the same. The result so obtained will be more reliable in comparison to the conclusion we draw without applying the principle of replication. The entire experiment can even be repeated several times for better results. Conceptually replication does not present any difficulty, but computationally it does. For example, if an experiment requiring a two-way analysis of variance is replicated, it will then require a three-way analysis of variance since replication itself may be a source of variation in the data. However, it should be remembered that replication is introduced in order to increase the precision of a study; that is to say, to increase the accuracy with which the main effects and interactions

can be estimated.

**(2)The Principle of Randomization:** The Principle of Randomization provides protection, when we conduct an experiment, against the effect of extraneous factors by randomization. In other words, this principle indicates that we should design or plan the experiment in such a way that the variations caused by extraneous factors can all be combined under the general heading of "chance." For instance, if we grow one variety of rice, say, in the first half of the parts of a field and the other variety is grown in the other half, then it is just possible that the soil fertility may be different in the first half in comparison to the other half. If this is so, our results would not be realistic. In such a situation, we may assign the variety of rice to be grown in different parts of the field on the basis of some random sampling technique i.e., we may apply randomization principle and protect ourselves against the effects of the extraneous factors (soil fertility differences in the given case). As such, through the application of the principle of randomization, we can have a better estimate of the experimental error.

**(3)Principle of Local Control:** The Principle of Local Control is another important principle of experimental designs. Under it the extraneous factor, the known source of variability, is made to vary deliberately over as wide a range as necessary and this needs to be done in such a way that the variability it causes can be measured and hence eliminated from the experimental error. This means that we should plan the experiment in a manner that we can perform a two-way analysis of variance, in which the total variability of the data is divided into three components attributed to treatments (varieties of rice in our case), the extraneous factor (soil fertility in our case) and experimental error. In other words, according to the principle of local control, we first divide the field into several homogeneous parts, known as blocks, and then each such block is divided into parts equal to the number of treatments. Then the treatments are randomly assigned to these parts of a block. Dividing the field into several homogenous parts is known as 'blocking'. In general, blocks are the levels at which we hold an extraneous factor fixed, so that we can measure its contribution to the total variability of the data by means of a two-way analysis of variance. In brief, through the principle of local control we can eliminate the variability due to extraneous factor(s) from the experimental error.

**PROCESS OF DEVELOPING A RESEARCH DESIGN**

1. Classify the intended outcome of what needs to be understood
2. Developing the research question
3. What needs to be measured
4. Select the population for the experiment
5. Identify the ideal data collection method
6. Construct Interrelated characteristics
7. Use correct analysis tools
8. Choose a channel for disseminating your findings

For students who are interested in reading about how to write a good research proposal to apply for the scholarship, must have a clear objective to persuade the admission committee. A research proposal is also required to contain a well-written study plan for submission.

CHAPTER FOUR

# THESIS RESEARCH PROPOSAL

**DEFINITION:**

A thesis research proposal is a planning document or statement of intent, which shows how a study would be executed. It is proposal submitted to an academic institution for the purpose of a higher degree. It is considered to important as it convey fovourably impression of the research project and enlighten the researcher's ability to handle the subject of the proposal. A proposal is usually developed in consultation with member of staff and it does not exceed 5000 written words. There are different points to be considered when preparing for a research proposal. These are:

- Research approach which may be of qualitative approach or quantitative approach
- Combination of qualitative preliminary study and quantitative main study.
- Collaboration with other researcher working bin related areas
- A good writing style
- Keeping a copies of draft proposal

**Components of research proposal**

i. **Title or Research topic:** This should be inshort phase explaining the subject of the proposal. It is usually constructed asa "problem" or "question" in need of of an answer.
ii. **Proponent:** This provide the name of the researcher, the name of the supervisor and collaborating researcher.

iii. **Background and context:** This gives a sketch or review of the topic to be handle, thus relating the topic to relevant literature. It includes a brief critical review of the literature relevant to the research topic. The background usually deals with issues like:

- Existing similar research relevant to your topic
- Relevant theoretical perspective
- Key ideas in your research approach
- Possible lines of inquiring to study

i. **Research question:** This can be derived from different areas such as personal interest, previous research, experimental concerns, theoretical concerns and world observation. There are different criteria for choosing research question. These are based on the following:

- Background value
- Research value
- Research interest
- Researcher's skills
- Resource accessibility
- Information accessibility

v. **Statement of problem:** This provides an explanation and creates an understanding of the existing situation on the subject matter. For example such as body mass index (BMI) and blood pressure; the problem statement will help to described BMI and blood pressure and also explain the relationship between the twovariables. Research question tends to address the following:

- Scientific importance of the problem
- Magnitude of the problem and how solution canbe provided to bring about development to the society
- Global and local complication
- Status of patient afflicted with the ailment
- Sex of patient with the ailment
- Age of patient with the ailment
- High incidence
- Nature of management

- Studied area or environment
- Degree of exposure etc

The problem there leads the researcher logically to the aims and general objectives of

The study, which is expected of the researcher to achieved.

vi. **Objectives:** The objectives can be classified into two section; the general objectives which provide a short statement of the development goal being pursued by the research and the specific objectives which indicate specific knowledge to be produced, groups or individual to be reached and certain forms of capacity to be reinforced. It is usually operational in nature.

vii. **Hypothesis:** This is a proposition that posits a relationships between two variables. Such statement is usually not expected and not confirmed. A hypothesisis a proposed explanation for a phenomenon. For a hypothesis to be a scientific hypothesis, the scientific method requires that one can test it. Scientists generally base scientific hypotheses on previous observations that cannot satisfactorily be explained with the available scientific theories. Hypothesis must possess the following characteristics:

- Hypothesis should be clear and precise.
- Hypothesis should be capable of being tested.
- Hypothesis should state relationship between variables, if it happens to be a relational hypothesis.
- Hypothesis should be limited in scope and must be specific.
- Hypothesis should be stated as far as possible in most simple terms .
- Hypothesis should be consistent with most known facts.
- Hypothesis should be amenable to testing within a reasonable time.
- Hypothesis must explain the facts that gave rise to the need for explanation.

Hypothesis are of two types;

i. **Null Hypothesis ($H_O$):** This is a statement indicating no significant differences between two variables.

ii. **Alternative Hypothesis($H_A$):** This is a statement indicating a significant differences between two variables.

Hypothesis tests are used in determining what outcomes of a study would lead to a acceptance or rejection of the null hypothesis for a pre-specified level of significance. In the Neyman-Pearson framework the process of distinguishing between the null hypothesis and the alternative hypothesis is aided by identifying two conceptual types of errors known as the type 1 and the type 2, and by specifying parametric limits on for instance; how much type 1 error will be permitted.

We may reject H0 when it is true, i.e. when we ought to have accept it. When this happens, we say that one has committed a type I error. Secondly, we may accept H0 when actually H0 is false. This again is called type II error. A test of hypothesis is considered good if both errors of judgments are minimized. This is not always possible. However in any particular situation, it is better to minimize the more serious error.

Suppose we have the null hypothesis that a particular drug is not poisonous, i.e. H0: drug is not poisonous.

Type I error: Reject H0 when it is true. This means that we assume the drug to be poisonous.

Type II error: Accept H0 when H0 is false. Here we try to minimize type II error and allow type I error to dominate.

viii. **Scope of study:** The study should be limited to a particular study area and the subject matter to be handled.

ix. **Significance of study:** this should explain how research will contribute to the body of knowledge within discipline, add value to previous knowledge or findings, add value to policy development, contribute to theory and add practical value in solving problem .

x. **Research methodology:** This is a set of systematic technique used in research. This simply means a guide to research and how it is conducted. It describes and analysis methods, throws more light on their limitations and resources, clarify their pre- suppositions and consequences, relating their potentialities to the twilight zone at the frontiers of knowledge.

Advantages of Research Methodology: The following are the advantages of research

methodology:

1. Advancement of wealth of human being
2. Provision of tools for carrying out the research
3. Develops a critical and scientific attitude, disciplined thinking to observations
4. Enrichment of the research process and provision of chance for in-depth study and understanding of the subject
5. Helps to inculcate the ability to evaluate and use research results with reasonable confidence and in decision making
6. Inculcates the ability to learn to read and think critically.

Research methodology is also refers to the process of data collection, data analysis and interpretation of data. This section provides the procedure to be undertaken in carrying out the study. The methodology used depends on the following:

1. **Used of Animal model:** Here, the methods to be considered includes;

- Animal Handling/timeline
- Collection and administration of material
- Experimental design(Grouping and treatment)
- Sample collection/procedure
- Determination of parameters/sample analysis
- Statistical analysis

2. **Used of questionnaire:** A questionnairc refers to a list of written questions which require the respondent to record the answers. The following terms are commonly used in questionnaire: a **respondent** is the person who answers question in a questionnaire. He can help to promote collection of data by cooperating with the interviewer or he can spoil the investigator's master-plan through his distorted answers, non-response, unnecessary enthusiasm to give answers that will please the interviewer. An observation unit, which can be defined as an identifiable physical entity on which such observations as measurements or attributes can be made is called enumeration unit. One or more variables may be observed on a unit. For example, in the pocket money survey, the students will be the respondent, he is also the unit on which to observe such attributes as the amount of pocket money, his age etc. However, in a study to find out the most popular brand of baby milk among babies of a specified age range, each baby is the observation unit. But the

respondent must necessarily be someone else like his parent or guardian, since the baby cannot answer questions himself. Having selected the topics to be included in the survey, we must formulate questions to cover each topic. The number, order and type of questions constitute the main elements of design of a questionnaire. The following are the guidelines for the designing of a good questionnaire:

(i) **Number of Questions:** The number of questions depends on the number of topics or variable being studied. Ideally they should be as few as possible. Too many questions, resulting in a lengthy and voluminous questionnaire may discourage a respondent from given the type of cooperation that he might have given with fewer questions. Repetition of questions should be avoided.

(ii) **Arrangement and Order of the Questions:** A well-arranged and well-ordered sequence of questions showing a logical and continuous flow of thought could be very helpful to the respondent.

(iii) **Simplicity and Clarity:** Simple, clear and unambiguous questions are more likely to have more meaningful responses than complicated and ambiguous questions. For example, a study in which one of the topics of interest is the marital status of the respondent, questions like "Married or Single" is not clear or that is ambiguous. Divorcees and widowers are left out. As an alternative may be: are you unmarried, married, widowed, divorced or separated? Where difficult or ambiguous questions are unavoidable, explanatory notes should be given so that the entire respondent interprets the questions in the same way. For instance, in a study involving families, the term 'family' should be defined. Does it consist of man, his wife, his children or does it include maids and houseboy etc.

(iv) **Open-ended and Closed-ended Questions:** Questions leading to definite answers are to be preferred to those that call for many possible answers which cannot be classified easily. The former type is said to be closed-ended, while the latter is open-ended. A question framed in such

a way as to demand only 'Yes', 'No' or 'don't know' is an example of closed-ended question.

Here, the method to be considered are as follows:

- Informed consent
- Ethical consideration
- Study area

- Study population/timeline
- Sampling study unit
- Inclusion criteria
- Exclusion criteria
- Statisticalanalysis

xi. **References:** This comprises of the list of consulted/relevant texts and it is usually at the of the research proposal. Reference indicate the works cited in the body of the proposal while bibliography refers to all relevant texts/materials to the subject of the investigation but not all cited in the body of the proposal.

**CRITERIA FOR ASSESSING AND APPROVING A CONCEPT PAPER OR FULL-BLOWN PROPOSAL**

Assessing and approving a research proposal is based on the following criteria:

1. Scientific merit: This is based on its relevance to the scientific world
2. Novelty
3. Quality and clarity
4. Identification of research problem
5. Focus of research objectives
6. Overall methodology
7. Research variability
8. Possible user linkage
9. General mastery of the subject matter
10. Research experience
11. Strength of collaboration

CHAPTER FIVE

# WRITING A THESIS

## INTRODUCTION

A thesis is simply a dissertation resulting from original research- especially when submitted for the award of a degree or diploma. It is aproduct of lengthy research done in academics. The emphasis of a thesis is on originality and research and this can be grouped into 3 major steps, namely:

1. **Starting research:** This involves the following;

- Clarifying research problem
- Establishing research objectives
- Formulating research question
- Outlining research method
- Conducting literature review
- Drafting a concept proposal

1. **Managing research data:** This is a term that describes the organization, storage, preservation, and sharing of data collected and used in a research project. It involves the everyday management of research data during the lifetime of a research project (for example, using consistent file naming conventions). It also involves decisions about how data will be preserved and shared after the project is completed (for example, depositing the data in a repository for long-term archiving and access).

   There are several of reasons why managing research data is important:

- Data, like journal articles and books, is a scholarly product.
- Data (especially digital data) is fragile and easily lost.

- There are growing research data requirements imposed by funders and publishers.
- Research data management saves time and resources in the long run.
- Good management helps to prevent errors and increases the quality of your analyses.
- Well-managed and accessible data allows others to validate and replicate findings.
- Research data management facilitates sharing of research data and, when shared, data can lead to valuable discoveries by others outside of the original research team.
- clarify your aims and objectives
- define your activities
- identify critical milestones
- ensure effective use of key resources
- define priorities
- increase the likelihood of successful completion.

3. **Reporting research:** This involve different parts

- **Prefatory parts**

- **Title fly page:** Only the title appears on this page. In case, it precedes the title page. Although, most of the reports don't have it.
- **Title page:** This should include four items; the title of the report, the name(s) of the persons for whom the report was prepared, the namesof person(s) who prepared it, and the date of release or presentation. It must be brief.
- **Abstract/ executive summary:** This entails five (5) elements such as (i) Aim/objective (ii) Brief background (iii) Result (iv) Conclusion (v) Recommendation
- **Table of contents:** This is based on the outline of the report. This should include first level subdivision but for short report, it is sufficient to include only the main divisions. Figures, tables and list of abbreviation usually followed after the table of contents.

- **Introduction :** The introduction comprises of background to study, statement of problem, justification of the study, objectives of the study, assumption, hypothesis or research question, scope of study, limitation of study, significant of study and definition of terms

- **Review of literature:** In reporting research at this current stage of the study, the need for detailed review of relevant materialonthe topic is paramount for the research toknow what other scholars in the field of study have done and how or where they were done or executed. This entails the information of other researcher tobuttress or jettison the data generated from the. In this way,the reviewed literature benefits the research conducted.It is organizedand written in reference to the specific objectives of the study

**Importance of literature review**

- It provides tentative solutions to the problem or tentative answers to the questions
- It indicates the theory on which the study is based; critiques and weigh studies as theory is built.
- It provides a conceptual frame work for the research.
- It provides an integrated overview of the area of study.
- It establishes a need for the research.
- It provides the rational for the hypothesis and variables

**Producing a quality literature review**

To produce a quality review of literature,the following must be practice

i. A survey of existing journal or article related to the area of study
ii. Citation of less than 10years paper
iii. Analysis of findings and critiques
iv. Integration of findings and critiques into the research work

- **Body of the thesis:** This run through two to three chapter (e.g. Materials &b method, Result analysis and Discussion, Conclusion, recommendation and references).
- **Appended parts:** This part entails data collection forms (questionnaire, checklist, interview guide or other forms), detailed calculations, general tables, and other supported materials like ethical consideration

**Stages of thesis writing**

1. Knowing what to write
2. Which approach or method do I use
3. Proposal drafting: It consists of the following outline;

- Title
- Background to study
- Statement of problem
- Objectives (General & Specific)
- Review of literature
- Materials and methodology
- References
- Cost implicationor budget

4. **Collection of data:** The methods of collecting primary and secondary data differ since primary data are to be originally collected, while in case of secondary data the nature of data collection work is merely that of compilation.

**Primary data**

Important ones are: (i) observation method, (ii) interview method, (iii) questionnaires, (iv) schedules, (v) other methods which include (a) warranty cards; (b) distributor audits; (c) pantry audits; (d) consumer panels; (e) using mechanical devices; (f) through projective techniques; (g) depth interviews, and (h) content analysis

**Secondary data**

Secondary data means data that are already available Usually published data are available in: (a)various publications of the central, state are local government (b) various publications of foreign governments or of international bodies and their subsidiary organizations (c) technical and trade journals (d) books, magazines and newspapers (e) reports and publications of various associations connected with business and industry, banks, stock exchanges, etc. (f) reports prepared by research scholars, universities, economists, etc. in different fields; (g) public records and statistics, historical documents, and other sources of published information.

5. **Note taking/documentation:** Here the following must be put into consideration.

- Style of writing: Here, the used of colloquialism, slngs, abbreviation must be avoided
- Layout
- Content
- Authority
- Referencing and sources
- Quotation
- Plagiarism

**PART OF THESIS**

There are different parts of a thesis. These include;

- Abstract/ executive summary
- Table of contents
- Introduction : The introduction comprises of background to study, statement of problem, justification of the study, objectives of the study, assumption, hypothesis or research question, scope of study, limitation of study, significant of study and definition of terms
- Literature review:
- Body of the thesis: This run through two to three chapter (e.g. Materials &b method, Result analysis and Discussion)
- Conclusion and recommendation
- The finished product
- The final version
- Defence or viva voce: This when the student is requested to defend or presentwhathe or she has done

CHAPTER SIX

# USEFUL TOOL FOR RESEARCH PURPOSE

## INTRODUCTION

One of the useful tools for research is the internet and intranet. The internet is a global network while the intranet is a local network of computer. The internet aids access to web materials or information loading and retrieval. Here, the network of a computer is of two types:

1. Wider Area network (WAN): This is a network spanning an area of farther than 5km or less.
2. Local Area Network: This is a network spanning an area of 5km or less.

### SEARCHING WEB INFORMATION

Web information or materials searching involving the use of the internet can be classified into two forms;

- High standard quality
- Low standard quality

Hence, when searching web materials to be incorporated into your research work, it is important to observe the following criteria:

1. The source of the information
2. The author (his qualification, background, address, email and webmaster or publisher)
3. The genuineness and scope of information
4. The date of first upload and updates and whether material is research oriented or not

5. The point of view, evidence of bias i.e. personal opinion, research report, whether the report is referred or edited.

Also, when searching web materials/Research publications and other reports and articles, it is important to consider the following:

- Keywords like the subject, author etc
- Boolean logic like AND, OR and NOT. For example; cats not rats; wealth and poverty; primary or secondary

**APPROACHES OF WEB SEARCHING**

Searching of web for information is of two approaches:

i. Approaches by visibility: This may lead researcher to visible web that is available with free access and invisible web that is not accessibility by query or restricted access e.g database, portal, non-textual file like PDF files
ii. Approaches by purpose: This may lead researcher to different pages like informative page, personal web page, political or interest group pages etc

# Conclusion

Research makes an effort to use methodical approaches to find answers to theoretical and practical concerns. Research is described as "studious inquiry or examination; especially: investigation or experimentation aimed at the discovery and interpretation of facts, revision of accepted theories or laws in the light of new facts, or practical application of such new or revised theories or laws" by Webster's Collegiate Dictionary. Some individuals view study as a transition from the known to the unknown. Actually, it's a journey of discovery. We all have the instinct to be curious, which is essential because it drives us to dig and gain a deeper understanding of the unknown when it confronts us. This curiosity is the source of all knowledge, and the process by which man learns about whatever the unknown is can be referred to as study. Through the use of scientific methods, research aims to find answers to open-ended questions. Finding the truth that is concealed and undiscovered as of yet is the major goal of study. Although each research project has a unique purpose, we can classify research objectives into the following major categories:

1. to become more familiar with a phenomenon or to gain new insights into it (studies with this goal are referred to as exploratory or formulative research studies);

2. to accurately depict the traits of a specific person, circumstance, or group of people (studies with this goal are referred to as descriptive research studies);

3. To ascertain how frequently something occurs or how it is connected to another thing (studies with this goal in mind are referred to as diagnostic research studies);

4. To examine a hypothesis regarding the existence of a causal link between two variables (these investigations are referred to as hypothesis-testing research studies).

9 798889 592600

Printed by Libri Plureos GmbH in Hamburg,
Germany